T0127516

COFFEE

COFFEE
A BOOK OF RECIPES

HELEN SUDELL

LORENZ BOOKS

This edition is published by Lorenz Books
an imprint of Anness Publishing Limited
Blaby Road, Wigston, Leicestershire LE18 4SE
info@anness.com
www.lorenzbooks.com; www.annesspublishing.com

© 2013 Anness Publishing Limited

If you like the images in this book and would like to
investigate using them for publishing, promotions
or advertising, please visit our website
www.practicalpictures.com for more information

A CIP catalogue record for this book is available from
The British Library

Publisher Joanna Lorenz
Editorial Director Helen Sudell
Designer Nigel Partridge
Illustrations Anna Koska

Jacket photography Janine Hosegood
Recipes by: Georgina Campbell, Joanna Farrow, Christine
France, Carole Handslip, Silvena Johan Lauta, Christine
McFadden, Ewa Michalik, Carol Pastor, Claire Ptak
Photographs by: Martin Brigdale, Nicki Dowey, Gus Filgate,
Will Heap, Amanda Heywood, William Lingwood,
Craig Robertson

COOK'S NOTES

• Bracketed terms are intended for American readers.

• For all recipes, quantities are given in both metric and
imperial measures and, where appropriate, in standard cups
and spoons. Follow one set of measures, but not a mixture,
because they are not interchangeable.

• Standard spoon and cup measures are level. 1 tsp = 5ml,
1 tbsp = 15ml, 1 cup = 250ml/8fl oz.

• Australian standard tablespoons are 20ml. Australian
readers should use 3 tsp in place of 1 tbsp for measuring
small quantities.

• American pints are 16fl oz/2 cups. American readers
should use 20fl oz/2.5 cups in place of 1 pint when
measuring liquids.

• Electric oven temperatures in this book are for
conventional ovens. When using a fan oven, the temperature
will probably need to be reduced by about
10–20°C/20–40°F. Since ovens vary, you should check with
your manufacturer's instruction book for guidance.

• The nutritional analysis given for each recipe is calculated
per portion (i.e. serving or item), unless otherwise stated.
If the recipe gives a range, such as Serves 4–6, then the
nutritional analysis will be for the smaller portion size,
i.e. 6 servings. The analysis does not include optional
ingredients, such as salt added to taste.

• Medium (US large) eggs are used unless otherwise stated.
• Unsalted butter is used unless otherwise stated.

PUBLISHER'S NOTE

CONTENTS

INTRODUCTION

In the history of food, in the West in particular, coffee is one of the youngsters; it has been known in Europe only since the end of the 17th century. There is little evidence to show how coffee was discovered, but it is known that it was enjoyed as a drink for centuries in the Middle East before the Venetians brought it to Europe. Here, coffee houses sprang up, frequented by the intelligentsia and the fashionable elite, who would spend hours drinking coffee and talking over the pressing issues of the day.

Despite its relative newness, coffee has become one of our favourite ingredients, loved not only as a beverage but also as an indispensable and delicious flavouring in all sorts of dishes from hot and cold desserts, cookies, cakes and bakes. As coffee has become an increasingly popular non-alcoholic beverage, there has also been a rise in its use as a key cooking ingredient.

Coffee can be grown only in tropical regions and once Europe acquired a taste for it, plants were taken to South American and Caribbean colonies and coffee growing quickly became established. These areas, with their slave labour, provided a large and cheap labour force. Today coffee is grown and exported from more than fifty countries around the world.

Below: The aroma of fresh coffee beans is hard to beat.

Above: Turkish coffee is usually served black in small cups.

There are essentially two types of coffee plant of significance. *Coffea arabica*, which grows on steep slopes and uplands, is considered by connoisseurs as the superior coffee, being rich and aromatic. *Coffea robusta* is grown less widely, but it is far easier to cultivate. It can cope with lower altitudes, making harvesting much easier and therefore cheaper. It has a more earthy flavour and is generally used for the cheaper varieties of fresh and instant coffee.

After harvesting, the coffee fruit (called the cherry) is left to ripen for six to eight months and the dried skins and pulp are then removed. Inside the fruit lie the pale coffee beans, which are sorted and graded and then exported, to be roasted by the country of import.

Below: Once brewed, coffee can be kept warm over a gentle heat for up to an hour.

The characteristics valued in coffee are good acidity (which provides sharpness), body and aroma. Most of the coffee sold today in shops is a number of different coffees, blended in order to combine or neutralize these characteristics.

In cooking, the same rich flavour and aroma can transform almost any cake or dessert. This book features many classic coffee cakes,

Above: Grinding your own coffee beans is extremely satisfying, and economical too.

bakes and dessert recipes, including Tiramisu and Mocha Sponge Cake, plus new combinations such as Frosted Coffee and Raspberry Terrine, and Gingered Coffee Meringues. All of them highlight the richness in flavour that coffee brings to a dish.

TYPES OF COFFEE

BRAZILIAN
Brazil is the world's largest coffee grower, producing many different grades of coffee, most of which are used for the manufacture of instant coffee.

COLOMBIAN
Another large exporter of coffee, Colombian beans are medium- or dark-roasted and have a heady aroma.

COSTA RICAN
Mountain-grown beans are known for their high acidity. However, the majority of beans produced here have a rich, smooth flavour and fragrance.

GUATEMALAN
Beans from the higher areas of Guatemala produce full-flavoured coffee and are known for their high acidity. Other regions produce beans that have a pleasant, but milder spiciness and consequently medium-roast is recommended.

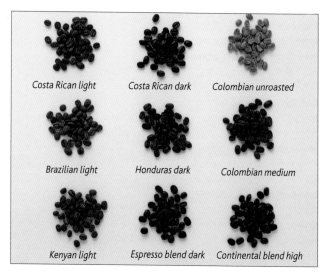

Costa Rican light *Costa Rican dark* *Colombian unroasted*

Brazilian light *Honduras dark* *Colombian medium*

Kenyan light *Espresso blend dark* *Continental blend high*

INDONESIAN
Best-known of these coffees are those from Java and Sumatra with their smooth flavour.

JAMAICAN
Thought by many to be the best coffee in the world, its wonderful aroma and delicate flavour are due to the natural sugars in the bean caramelizing during roasting.

Above: A selection of coffee beans: darker beans have a more intense flavour.

KENYAN
The Kenyan peaberry produces single round beans and is famed for its good flavour and acidity. This coffee is considered so fine that it is rarely blended and should be drunk black to enjoy it fully.

ROASTING COFFEE

The length of time that coffee is roasted gives a different taste.
Light roast: Suitable for mild coffees with a delicate aroma and flavour that would be lost with stronger roasting.
Medium roast: The best roast for coffees with a well-defined character. It gives a stronger flavour yet is still suitable for drinking black or with milk.
Full or Dark Roast: This gives a strong aroma and a fullbodied slighty bitter flavour.
High or Continental Roast: This accentuates the strong bitter aspects of coffee.

GRINDING COFFEE

Coffee is ground to various degrees – from coarse through to very finely ground, which is the best choice for espresso. The finer the grind means that there is a greater surface area for the water to filter through, making a stronger coffee. The grinding process generates heat that intensifies the flavour of the coffee beans.

INSTANT COFFEE

Made from coffee beans that have been brewed into a concentrate, this is sold in granular or powder form. Coffee bags are also available.

COFFEE ESSENCE

Useful for flavouring cakes and desserts. However, be sure to buy pure coffee essence and not a mix of chicory and coffee.

Below: The main coffee-making ingredients and flavourings.

COFFEE LIQUEUR

The best-known coffee liqueur is Tia Maria, a Jamaican rum liqueur made with coffee extracts and spices. Kahlúa is a rum-based coffee liqueur from Mexico.

SYRUPS FOR FLAVOURING COFFEE

There are many flavours to choose from, including vanilla, caramel, cinnamon, apple, hazelnut and Irish cream. Add to freshly brewed coffee.

Coffee bag

Turkish pulverized

Coffee essence

Fine ground espresso

Instant granules

Coarse ground coffee

Syrup for flavouring coffee

Instant espresso

Chocolate-covered coffee beans

Coffee liqueur

COOKING WITH COFFEE

MAKING FRESH COFFEE

It is important to choose the correct grind of coffee to suit the method of brewing. The finer the grain, the greater the surface area that is exposed to the water and the slower the water will run through it. Consequently the coffee will be more full-bodied and stronger.

Coffee machines are designed for a particular grind of coffee and if this is not right the resulting coffee will be either weak and thin-tasting if the grains are too coarse, or bitter and harsh if the grind is too fine. If buying a coffee grinder, choose one that can be adjusted according to the grind required. Coarse-ground grains should be the consistency of granulated sugar, pulverized grains should appear similar to the consistency of icing (confectioners') sugar, with the others coming on a scale in between.

BUYING COFFEE

For the best flavour, buy coffee beans from a good coffee shop. They will be freshly roasted and should be used within a week. Freshly roasted beans can be frozen for up to 6 months, with little or no loss of flavour. If purchasing from supermarkets, buy the vacuum-packed coffees, which will last, unopened, until the use-by date on the packet. Once opened, however, all coffee, and ground

Above: Once open, ground coffee should be kept in a sealed container in the refrigerator or other cool place.

coffee particularly, will lose its flavour quickly. Consequently, buy only small amounts of coffee beans at a time.

Coffee beans and ground coffee should be stored in an airtight container in a cool place. The exception are espresso blends: the dark-roasted beans react adversely to chilling, as the oil in the beans tends to coagulate.

THE RIGHT GRIND FOR EACH BREWING METHOD
- Jug and Percolator: coarse
- Plunger or Cafetiere: medium
- Glass Balloon/Vacuum: medium fine
- Neapolitan Flip Pots: medium
- Filter/Drip: fine
- Moka Espresso Pots: espresso
- Ibrik (for Turkish coffee): pulverized

COFFEE BREWING TIPS

• Use fresh, cold water.

• Never use boiling water: water should be just off the boil, at 92-96°C/198-205°F.

• Drink as soon as possible after brewing.

• Always keep coffee equipment scrupulously clean.

• The quantity of coffee required for brewed coffee will depend partly on the brewing method and partly on taste. As a rule, however, use 25-30g/1½-2 tbsp ground coffee per cup.

• For Turkish coffee, 1 heaped teaspoon each of coffee and sugar per cup will make a strong coffee.

• In recipes calling for brewed coffee, make the coffee up according to your preferred method, or reserve a little coffee from breakfast or lunch. Since this coffee will be blended with other ingredients and will frequently be reheated as part of the recipe process, the coffee does not have to be freshly made.

USING A CAFETIÈRE (PRESS POT)

For this method use only coarse or medium grinds or the coffee will be cloudy.

1 Preheat the glass cylinder by filling it with hot water; while more water is heating for brewing, pour the water from the glass cylinder into a measuring jug and calculate the amount of coffee needed, working at 55g/10 tbsp per 1 litre/33fl oz/4 cups of water.

2 Dry the glass and place the dry coffee in it. When the water for brewing is almost at boiling point (just before it boils or left for a few moments afterwards), pour it over the dry coffee.

3 Stir it very well with a large spoon. The more freshly ground the coffee, the more it has a tendency to float and seems more resistant to saturation by the water, so stir thoroughly to incorporate all the dry coffee.

4 Prop the sieve device, with the lid above it, just inside the top of the cylinder for about four minutes. This will stop cool air from leaking down into the pot and will keep the water as hot as possible. When the brewing time is up, hold the lid down with one hand to stabilize the plunger shaft and, with the other hand, slowly and carefully push down the plunger. Serve the coffee as soon as possible.

COFFEE DRINKS

IRISH COFFEE
A good Irish coffee is an exercise in contrast and a lovely treat.

Serves 1
25ml/1½ tbsp Irish whiskey
about 150ml/¼ pint/⅔ cup hot strong black coffee
demerara (raw) sugar, to taste
about 50ml/2fl oz/¼ cup lightly whipped chilled cream

Measure the whiskey into a strong glass. Pour in freshly made black coffee to come to about 1cm/½ in from the top.

Below: Irish Coffee.

Sweeten to taste and stir vigorously to dissolve the sugar and create a small whirlpool in the glass. Top the coffee with the lightly whipped cream, poured over the back of the teaspoon. It will settle on the top to make a distinct layer in creamy contrast to the dark coffee underneath.

ESPRESSO CRUSH
This iced coffee combines frozen granita with ice cream.

Makes 4 glasses
75ml/5 tbsp ground espresso coffee
75g/3oz/scant ½ cup caster (superfine) sugar
300g/11oz vanilla ice cream
75ml/5 tbsp milk or soya milk

Put the coffee in a cafetière (press pot), add 750ml/1¼ pints/3 cups boiling water and leave to infuse for 5 minutes. Plunge the cafetière and pour the coffee into a shallow

freezer container. Stir in the sugar until dissolved. Leave to cool completely, then cover and freeze for about 2 hours.

Using a fork, break up the ice crystals, stirring them into the centre of the container. Re-freeze until the mixture is slushy around the edges. Repeat forking and stirring once or twice more until the mixture is completely slushy and there is no liquid remaining. Re-freeze until ready to use.

Put the ice cream and milk in a blender or food processor and

Below: Espresso Crush.

process until thick and smooth. To serve, spoon a little into the base of each glass and sprinkle with a layer of the granita. Repeat layering until the glasses are full. Serve immediately.

CINNAMON ICED COFFEE
A classy cool drink, perfect to pick you up at any time of day.

Makes 2 large glasses
5ml/1 tsp ground cinnamon
400ml/14fl oz/1²/₃ cups full cream (whole) milk
40g/1½oz/3 tbsp caster (superfine) sugar
300ml/½ pint/1¼ cups strong cold espresso coffee
ice cubes
cinnamon sticks, to serve

Put the cinnamon and 100ml/3½fl oz/ scant ½ cup of the milk in a small pan with the sugar. Bring the milk slowly to the boil then remove from the heat and leave to cool.

Turn the cinnamon milk into a large jug (pitcher) or bowl.

Above: Cinnamon Iced Coffee.

Add the remaining milk and the coffee and whisk well, until frothy. Pour into glasses with ice and serve with cinnamon sticks for stirrers.

AFTER-DINNER COFFEE
A superb end to a meal. Kahlúa is a Mexican coffee liqueur.

Serves 4
50g/2oz/⅓ cup dark-roast ground coffee
120ml/4fl oz/½ cup tequila
120ml/4fl oz/½ cup Kahlúa liqueur
5ml/1 tsp natural vanilla extract
25g/1oz/2 tbsp soft dark brown

sugar
150ml/¼ pint/²/₃ cup double (heavy) cream (optional)

Put the ground coffee in a cafetière (press pot), pour 475ml/16fl oz/2 cups boiling water and leave until the coffee grounds settle at the bottom.

Plunge the cafetière and pour the strained coffee into a clean heatproof jug. Add the tequila, Kahlúa and vanilla essence to the coffee and stir well to mix. Add the sugar and continue to stir until it has dissolved. Pour the mixture into coffee cups and add the cream, if using.

Below: After-dinner Coffee.

COFFEE COOKIES & SMALL BAKES

COFFEE-FLAVOURED CAKES CAN BE SERVED FOR
MORNING BREAKS OR FOR AFTERNOON
DELIGHTS. THEY CAN BE AS SIMPLE OR EXOTIC AS
YOU LIKE: EITHER WAY THE RICH FLAVOUR OF
COFFEE ADDS A SOPHISTICATED TOUCH

VIENNESE WHIRLS

These crisp, melt-in-the-mouth piped biscuits are filled with a creamy coffee buttercream.
They are only small in size so you can treat yourself to more than one.

Makes 20

175g/6oz/12 tbsp butter
50g/2oz/½ cup icing
  (confectioners') sugar
2.5ml/½ tsp vanilla extract
115g/4oz/1 cup plain (all-
  purpose) flour
50g/2oz/½ cup cornflour
  (cornstarch)
icing (confectioners') sugar and
  cocoa powder, to dust

For the filling

15ml/1 tbsp ground coffee
60ml/4 tbsp single (light) cream
75g/3oz/6 tbsp butter, softened
115g/4oz/1 cup icing
  (confectioners') sugar, sifted

Preheat the oven to 180°C/350°F/Gas 4. Cream together the butter, icing sugar and vanilla extract until light. Sift in the flour and cornflour and mix in until smooth.

Using two tablespoons, spoon the mixture into a piping bag fitted with a 1cm/½in fluted nozzle.

Pipe small rosettes well apart on greased baking sheets. Bake in the oven for 12–15 minutes until golden. Transfer to a wire rack to cool.

To make the filling, put the coffee in a bowl. Heat the cream to near-boiling and pour it over. Infuse for 4 minutes, then strain through a fine sieve. Beat the butter, icing sugar and coffee-flavoured cream until light. Use to sandwich the biscuits in pairs. Dust with icing sugar and cocoa powder.

Energy 210kcal/877kJ; Protein 2.2g;
Carbohydrate 21.3g, of which sugars
11.2g; Fat 13.5g, of which saturates 7.6g;
Cholesterol 22mg; Calcium 28mg; Fibre
0.8g; Sodium 64mg.

PECAN TOFFEE AND COFFEE SHORTBREAD

Coffee shortbread is topped with pecan-studded toffee. Cornflour (cornstarch) gives it a crumbly light texture, but plain (all-purpose) flour can be used if you like.

Makes 20

15ml/1 tbsp ground coffee
15ml/1 tbsp near-boiling water
115g/4oz/8 tbsp butter,
    softened
30ml/2 tbsp smooth peanut
    butter
75g/3oz/scant ½ cup caster
    (superfine) sugar
75g/3oz/²⁄₃ cup cornflour
    (cornstarch)
185g/6½oz/1²⁄₃ cups plain (all-
    purpose) flour

For the topping

175g/6oz/12 tbsp butter
175g/6oz/¾ cup soft light
    brown sugar
30ml/2 tbsp golden (light corn)
    syrup
175g/6oz/1 cup shelled pecan
    nuts, roughly chopped

Energy 267kcal/1112kJ; Protein 1.9g;
Carbohydrate 25.5g, of which sugars
14.9g; Fat 18.2g, of which saturates 8.1g;
Cholesterol 31mg; Calcium 28mg; Fibre
0.7g; Sodium 95mg.

Preheat the oven to 180°C/350°F/Gas 4. Lightly grease and line the base of a 18 x 28cm/7 x 11in sandwich tin (layer pan) with baking parchment.

Put the ground coffee in a small bowl and pour the hot water over. Leave to infuse for 4 minutes, then strain through a fine sieve (strainer).

Cream the butter, peanut butter, sugar and coffee together until light. Sift (strain) the cornflour and flour together and mix in to make a smooth dough.

Press into the base of the tin and prick all over with a fork. Bake for 20 minutes.

To make the topping, put the butter, sugar and syrup in a pan and heat until melted. Bring to the boil. Allow to simmer for 5 minutes, then stir in the chopped nuts. Spread the topping over the base. Leave in the tin until cold, then cut into fingers. Remove from the tin and serve.

COFFEE SPONGE DROPS

These taste divine on their own, but are even better with a filling made by mixing low fat soft cheese with drained and chopped preserved stem ginger.

Makes 12
50 g/2 oz/½ cup plain (all-
    purpose) flour
15 ml/1 tbsp instant coffee
    powder
2 eggs
75 g/3 oz/6 tbsp caster
    (superfine) sugar

For the filling
115 g/4 oz/½ cup low fat soft
    cheese
40 g/1½ oz/¼ cup chopped
    preserved stem ginger

Energy 33kcal/138kJ; Protein 1.5g;
Carbohydrate 5.2g, of which sugars 3.6g;
Fat 0.9g, of which saturates 0.4g;
Cholesterol 17mg; Calcium 13mg; Fibre
0.1g; Sodium 27mg.

Preheat the oven to 190°C/375°F/Gas 5. Line two baking sheets with non-stick baking parchment. Make the filling by beating together the soft cheese and stem ginger. Chill until required. Sift (strain) the flour and instant coffee powder together.

Combine the eggs and caster sugar in a bowl. Beat with a hand-held electric whisk until thick and mousse-like (when the whisk is lifted a trail should remain on the surface of the mixture for at least 15 seconds).

Carefully add the sifted flour and coffee mixture and gently fold in with a metal spoon, being careful not to knock out any air.

Spoon the mixture into a piping bag fitted with a 1 cm/½ in plain nozzle. Pipe 4 cm/1½ in rounds on the baking sheets. Bake for 12 minutes. Cool on a wire rack. Sandwich together with the filling.

BLACK RUSSIAN COOKIES

The ingredients of the famous cocktail – coffee and vodka – flavour these fabulous cookies.
If making a batch for children then simply replace the vodka with water.

Makes 16

30ml/2 tbsp ground espresso or
other strong-flavoured coffee
60ml/4 tbsp near-boiling milk
115g/4oz/8 tbsp butter
115g/4oz/½ cup soft light
brown sugar
1 egg
225g/8oz/2 cups plain (all-
purpose) flour
5ml/1 tsp baking powder
pinch of salt

For the icing

115g/4oz/1 cup icing
(confectioners') sugar
about 25ml/1½ tbsp vodka

Energy 168kcal/706kJ; Protein 2g;
Carbohydrate 26.2g, of which sugars
15.5g; Fat 6.5g, of which saturates 3.9g;
Cholesterol 27mg; Calcium 35mg; Fibre
0.4g; Sodium 51mg.

Preheat the oven to 180°C/350°F/Gas 4. Put the coffee in a small bowl and pour the hot milk over. Infuse for 4 minutes, strain and cool.

Cream the butter and sugar together until light and fluffy. Gradually beat in the egg. Sift the flour, baking powder and salt together and fold in with the coffee-flavoured milk to make a fairly stiff mixture.

Place dessertspoonfuls of the mixture on greased baking sheets, spacing them slightly apart to allow room for a little spreading. Bake the cookies for 15 minutes, until lightly browned. Cool on a wire rack.

To make the icing, mix the icing sugar and enough vodka together to make a thick icing. Spoon into a small greaseproof paper piping bag.

Snip off the end of the piping bag and lightly drizzle the icing over the top of each cookie. Allow the icing to set before serving.

COFFEE AND CHOCOLATE CAKES

*This recipe hails from Bucharest where you will see people eating the cakes in coffee shops. These
moist cakes are made with walnuts and topped with chocolate and mascarpone.*

Makes 12
*175g/6oz/1½ cups self-raising
    (self-rising) flour
175g/6oz/¾ cup butter
175g/6oz/scant 1 cup caster
    (superfine) sugar
3 large (US extra large) eggs
45ml/3 tbsp espresso coffee
75g/3oz/½ cup walnuts,
    roughly chopped*

For the syrup
*50g/2oz/¼ cup soft light brown
    sugar
30ml/2 tbsp hot espresso coffee*

For the topping
*50g/2oz milk chocolate
115g/4oz/½ cup mascarpone,
    at room temperature
12 walnut halves, to decorate*

Energy 339kcal/1414kJ; Protein 5.4g;
Carbohydrate 33.9g, of which sugars 22.7g;
Fat 21.1g, of which saturates 10.3g;
Cholesterol 86mg; Calcium 56mg; Fibre
0.7g; Sodium 134mg.

Preheat the oven to 180°C/350°F/ Gas 4. Put 12 paper cake cases into
a bun or muffin tin (pan). Put the flour into a large bowl and add the
butter, sugar and eggs. Whisk together until smooth and fluffy. Fold in
the coffee and chopped nuts.

Spoon the mixture into the paper cases. Bake for 15 minutes, or until
risen and firm to the touch.

While the cakes are in the oven, make the syrup. Dissolve the sugar
in the espresso coffee.

As soon as the cakes come out of the oven, pierce them in several
places with a skewer and drizzle the coffee syrup over the top. Leave
to cool.

To make the topping, melt the chocolate in a heatproof bowl over
a pan of gently simmering water, then leave to cool slightly.

Whisk the mascarpone and melted chocolate together until smooth.
Spread over the cakes, decorate each with a walnut half and serve
immediately.

COFFEE MUFFINS WITH TOFFEE FUDGE FROSTING

With a dense texture and complex flavours these coffee muffins are truly a cake to savour. The rich and sweet smooth toffee frosting is a contrast to the grainy textured cake.

Makes 10 standard muffins

100ml/3½fl oz/scant ½ cup
   single (light) cream
10ml/2 tsp instant coffee granules
15ml/1 tbsp fine-ground coffee
175g/6oz/¾ cup butter, softened
175g/6oz/¾ cup soft light
   brown sugar
2 eggs
100g/3¾oz/scant 1 cup spelt
   flour
100g/3¾oz/scant 1 cup self-
   raising (self-rising) flour

For the frosting

75g/3oz/6 tbsp butter
75g/3oz/scant ½ cup soft light
   brown sugar
15ml/1 tbsp golden (light corn)
   syrup
5ml/1 tsp instant coffee granules
130g/4½oz/generous 1 cup
   icing (confectioners') sugar,
   sifted
5ml/1 tsp lemon juice
candy-coated coffee beans, to
   decorate

Place the cream, instant and ground coffees in a small pan and bring to the boil. Remove from the heat. Set aside to cool.

Preheat the oven to 180°C/350°F/Gas 4. Line the cups of a muffin tin (pan) with paper cases.

In a mixing bowl, beat the butter and sugar until light and creamy, then gradually beat in the eggs one at a time. Beat in the cooled coffee mixture until just combined.

Sift the two flours into the creamed mixture and fold in until just combined. Do not overmix.

Three-quarters fill the paper cases with the batter. Bake for 20–25 minutes. Leave to stand for 5 minutes in the tin before turning out on to a wire rack to go completely cold.

To make the frosting, melt 50g/2oz/¼ cup of the butter with the sugar and golden syrup in a pan over a low heat, stirring occasionally.

Dissolve the coffee in 50ml/2fl oz/¼ cup boiling water and add to the ingredients in the pan. Bring slowly to the boil, stirring frequently, then simmer for 3 minutes, stirring once or twice. Remove from the heat and pour into a large bowl.

Whisk in the icing sugar, then the lemon juice and remaining butter. Beat until smooth. Stand the bowl in iced water and stir until the mixture thickens. Spread on to the tops of the muffins. Decorate with candy-coated coffee beans.

Energy 441kcal/1846kJ; Protein 3.6g; Carbohydrate 56.7g, of which sugars 41.5g; Fat 23.8g, of which saturates 15.1g; Cholesterol 101mg; Calcium 56mg; Fibre 1.5g; Sodium 213mg.

COFFEE CAKES

ADD COFFEE TO ANY SPONGE CAKE, SWISS ROLL
OR CHEESECAKE AND YOU WILL TRANSFORM EVEN
THE SIMPLEST RECIPE INTO A MEMORABLE AFTER-
NOON TREAT OR FABULOUS CELEBRATORY
CREATION FOR A SPECIAL OCCASION

COCONUT COFFEE CAKE

Coconut and coffee are natural partners, as these little squares of iced cake display perfectly.
They are light and airy and will prove very difficult to resist.

Serves 9

45ml/3 tbsp ground coffee
75ml/5 tbsp near-boiling milk
*25g/1oz/2 tbsp caster
(superfine) sugar*
*175g/6oz/²⁄₃ cup golden (corn
oil) syrup*
75g/3oz/6 tbsp butter
*40g/1½oz/½ cup desiccated
coconut*
*175g/6oz/1½ cups plain (all-
purpose) flour*
*2.5ml/½ tsp bicarbonate of
soda (baking soda)*
2 eggs, lightly beaten

For the icing

*115g/4oz/8 tbsp butter,
softened*
*225g/8oz/2 cups icing
(confectioners') sugar, sifted*
*25g/1oz/¹⁄₃ cup shredded or
flaked coconut, toasted*

Energy 418kcal/1756kJ; Protein 3.7g;
Carbohydrate 59.7g, of which sugars
44.9g; Fat 20g, of which saturates 13g;
Cholesterol 90mg; Calcium 57mg; Fibre
1g; Sodium 225mg.

Preheat the oven to 160°C/325°F/Gas 3. Grease and line the base of a 20cm/8in square tin (pan).

Put the ground coffee in a small bowl and pour the hot milk over. Leave to infuse for 4 minutes, then strain. Heat the sugar, golden syrup, butter and desiccated coconut in a pan, stirring until completely melted. Sift the flour and bicarbonate of soda together and stir into the mixture, along with the eggs and 45ml/3 tbsp of the coffee-flavoured milk.

Spoon the mixture into the prepared tin and level the top. Bake for 40–50 minutes. Cool the cake in the tin for 10 minutes, then run a knife around the tin to loosen. Turn out and cool on a wire rack.

To make the icing, beat the butter with the icing sugar and remaining coffee milk to give a soft consistency. Spread over the top of the cake and decorate with toasted coconut. Cut into 5cm/2in squares to serve.

MOCHA SPONGE CAKE

The Yemeni city of Mocha was once considered to be the coffee capital of the world, and still produces a coffee that tastes a little like chocolate.

Serves 10

25ml/1½ tbsp strong-flavoured ground coffee
175ml/6fl oz/¾ cup milk
115g/4oz/8 tbsp butter
115g/4oz/½ cup soft light brown sugar
1 egg, lightly beaten
185g/6½oz/1²⁄₃ cups self-raising (self-rising) flour
5ml/1 tsp bicarbonate of soda (baking soda)
60ml/4 tbsp creamy liqueur, such as Baileys or Irish Velvet

For the glossy chocolate icing

200g/7oz plain (semisweet) chocolate, broken into pieces
75g/3oz/6 tbsp unsalted butter, cubed
120ml/4fl oz/½ cup double (heavy) cream

Energy 444kcal/1853kJ; Protein 4.2g; Carbohydrate 41.2g, of which sugars 27.3g; Fat 29.7g, of which saturates 17.6g; Cholesterol 78mg; Calcium 112mg; Fibre 1.1g; Sodium 206mg.

Preheat the oven to 180°C/350°F/Gas 4. Grease and line a 18cm/7in round fixed-base cake tin (pan) with baking parchment.

To make the cake, put the coffee in a jug (pitcher). Heat the milk to near-boiling and pour over. Leave to infuse for 4 minutes, then strain through a sieve (strainer) and cool.

Gently melt the butter and sugar until dissolved. Pour into a bowl and cool for 2 minutes, then stir in the egg.

Sift (strain) the flour over the mixture and fold in. Blend the bicarbonate of soda with the coffee-flavoured milk and stir into the mixture.

Pour into the tin, smooth the surface, and bake for 40 minutes, until well-risen and firm. Cool in the tin for about 10 minutes. Spoon the liqueur over the cake and leave until cold. Loosen the edges with a palette knife and turn out on to a wire rack.

To make the icing, place the broken chocolate in a bowl over a pan of barely simmering water until melted. Remove from the heat and stir in the butter and cream until smooth. Allow to cool before coating the top and sides of the cake, using a palette knife. Leave until set.

COFFEE AND MINT CREAM CAKE

Ground almonds give this buttery coffee sponge a moist texture and delicate flavour. It's sandwiched together with a generous filling of crème de menthe buttercream.

Serves 8

15ml/1 tbsp ground coffee
25ml/1½ tbsp near-boiling water
175g/6oz/12 tbsp butter, softened
175g/6oz/scant 1 cup caster (superfine) sugar
225g/8oz/2 cups self-raising (self-rising) flour, sifted
50g/2oz/½ cup ground almonds
3 eggs
sprigs of fresh mint, to decorate

For the filling

50g/2oz/4 tbsp butter
115g/4oz/1 cup icing (confectioners') sugar, sifted, plus extra for dusting
30ml/2 tbsp crème de menthe liqueur

Energy 508kcal/2127kJ; Protein 6.5g;
Carbohydrate 59.6g, of which sugars
38.5g; Fat 28.8g, of which saturates
16.1g; Cholesterol 136mg; Calcium
148mg; Fibre 1.3g; Sodium 341mg.

Preheat the oven to 180°C/350°F/Gas 4. Lightly grease and base line two 18cm/7in shallow round cake tins (pans) with baking parchment.

Put the coffee in a bowl and pour the hot water over. Leave to infuse for about 4 minutes, then strain through a sieve (strainer).

Put the butter, sugar, flour, almonds, eggs and coffee in a large bowl. Beat well for 1 minute until blended. Divide the mixture evenly between the tins and level off. Bake for 25 minutes until well-risen and firm to the touch. Leave in the tins for 5 minutes, then turn out on to a wire rack to cool.

To make the filling, cream the butter, icing sugar and crème de menthe liqueur together in a bowl until light and fluffy.

Remove the lining paper from the sponges and sandwich together with the filling.

Generously dust the top with icing sugar and place on a serving plate. Scatter with the fresh mint leaves just before serving.

COFFEE AND WALNUT SWISS ROLL

Coffee and walnuts have a natural affinity. Here they appear together in a light and fluffy sponge enclosing a smooth and luxurious orange liqueur cream.

Serves 6

10ml/2 tsp ground coffee, e.g. mocha orange-flavoured
15ml/1 tbsp near-boiling water
3 eggs
75g/3oz/scant ½ cup caster (superfine) sugar, plus extra for dusting
75g/3oz/⅔ cup self-raising (self-rising) flour
50g/2oz/½ cup toasted walnuts, finely chopped

For the Cointreau cream

115g/4oz/generous ½ cup caster (superfine) sugar
50ml/2fl oz/¼ cup cold water
2 egg yolks
115g/4oz/8 tbsp butter, softened
15ml/1 tbsp Cointreau

> **COOK'S TIP**
> Decorate the roll with piped whipped cream and walnuts, if you like.

Preheat the oven to 200°C/400°F/Gas 6. Grease and line a 33 x 23cm/13 x 9in Swiss roll tin (jelly roll pan) with non-stick baking parchment.

Put the coffee in a bowl and pour the hot water over. Leave to infuse for about 4 minutes, then strain through a sieve (strainer).

Whisk the eggs and sugar together in a large bowl until pale and thick. Sift the flour over the mixture and fold in with the coffee and walnuts. Turn into the tin and bake for 10–12 minutes, until springy to the touch.

Turn out on a piece of baking parchment sprinkled with caster sugar, peel the non-stick baking parchment off the sponge and cool for about 2 minutes. Trim the edges then roll up from one of the short ends, with the baking parchment where the filling will be. Leave to cool.

To make the filling, heat the sugar in the water over a low heat until dissolved. Boil rapidly until the syrup reaches 105°C/220°F on a sugar thermometer. Pour the syrup over the egg yolks, whisking all the time, until thick and mousse-like. Gradually add the butter, then whisk in the orange liqueur. Leave to cool and thicken.

Unroll the sponge and spread with the Cointreau cream. Re-roll and place on a serving plate seam-side down. Dust with extra caster sugar and chill in the refrigerator until ready to serve.

Energy 357kcal/1489kJ; Protein 4.1g; Carbohydrate 31.9g, of which sugars 28.7g; Fat 24.6g, of which saturates 11.9g; Cholesterol 125mg; Calcium 43mg; Fibre 0.4g; Sodium 153mg.

IRISH COFFEE CHEESECAKE

The flavours of whiskey, coffee and ginger go well together, but you can ring the changes by using almond or digestive biscuits (graham crackers) for the base of this cheesecake.

Serves 8

45ml/3 tbsp ground coffee
1 vanilla pod
250ml/8fl oz/1 cup single (light) cream
15ml/1 tbsp powdered gelatine
45ml/3 tbsp cold water
450g/1lb/2 cups curd (farmer's) cheese, at room temperature
60ml/4 tbsp whiskey liqueur
115g/4oz/½ cup soft light brown sugar
150ml/¼ pint/⅔ cup whipping cream

To decorate

150ml/¼ pint/⅔ cup whipping cream
chocolate-covered coffee beans
cocoa, for dusting

For the base

150g/5oz gingernut (gingersnap) biscuits, finely crushed
25g/1oz/¼ cup toasted almonds, chopped
75g/3oz/6 tbsp butter, melted

To make the base, mix together the crushed gingernut biscuits, toasted almonds and melted butter and press firmly into the base of a 20cm/8in loose-based tin (pan). Chill in the refrigerator.

Heat the coffee, vanilla and single cream in a pan to near-boiling point. Cover and leave to infuse for 15 minutes. Strain through a fine sieve (strainer). Sprinkle the gelatine over the water in a bowl and leave for 5 minutes. Place over a pan of simmering water until dissolved. Stir into the coffee cream.

Mix the curd cheese, liqueur and sugar together, then gradually blend in the coffee cream. Leave until just beginning to set.

Beat the whipping cream until soft peaks form, and fold into the coffee mixture. Spoon into the tin and chill for 3 hours, until set.

To decorate, whisk the whipping cream until soft peaks form and spread lightly over the top. Chill for at least 30 minutes, then transfer to a serving plate. Decorate with chocolate-covered coffee beans and dust with cocoa.

Energy 506kcal/2110kJ; Protein 14.2g; Carbohydrate 36.2gm, of which sugars 27.7g; Fat 33g, of which saturates 19g; Cholesterol 77.1mg; Calcium 167.4mg; Fibre 0.5g; Sodium 175mg.

STICKY COFFEE AND GINGER PUDDING

This coffee-capped feather-light sponge is made with breadcrumbs and ground almonds. Serve with creamy custard or scoops of vanilla ice cream.

Serves 4

30ml/2 tbsp soft light brown
  sugar
25g/1oz/2 tbsp preserved stem
  ginger, chopped
30ml/2 tbsp mild ground coffee
75ml/5 tbsp preserved stem
  ginger syrup (from a jar of
  stem ginger)
115g/4oz/generous ½ cup
  caster (superfine) sugar
3 eggs, separated
25g/1oz/¼ cup plain (all-
  purpose) flour
5ml/1 tsp ground ginger
65g/2½oz/generous 1 cup fresh
  white breadcrumbs
25g/1oz/¼ cup ground
  almonds

Energy 382Kcal/1617kJ; Protein 9.7g;
Carbohydrate 70.6g, of which sugars
53.5g; Fat 8.9g, of which saturates 1.7g;
Cholesterol 171g; Calcium 93mg; Fibre
1g; Sodium 240mg.

Preheat the oven to 180°C/350°F/Gas 4. Grease and line the base of a 750ml/1¼ pint/3 cup ovenproof bowl, then sprinkle in the soft light brown sugar and chopped preserved stem ginger.

Put the ground coffee in a small bowl. Heat the ginger syrup until almost boiling; pour into the coffee. Stir well and leave for 4 minutes. Pour through a fine sieve (strainer) into the ovenproof bowl.

Beat half the caster sugar and egg yolks until light and fluffy. Sift the flour and ground ginger together and fold into the egg mixture with the breadcrumbs and ground almonds.

Whisk the egg whites until stiff, then gradually whisk in the remaining caster sugar. Fold into the mixture, half at a time. Spoon into the bowl and smooth the top.

Cover the bowl with a piece of pleated greased baking parchment and secure with string. Bake for 40 minutes, or until the sponge is firm to the touch. Turn out and serve immediately.

COFFEE CRÊPES WITH PEACHES AND CREAM

Juicy golden peaches and cream conjure up the sweet taste of summer. Here they are delicious as the filling for these light coffee crêpes.

Serves 6

75g/3oz/²/₃ cup plain (all-purpose) flour
25g/1oz/¹/₄ cup buckwheat flour
1.5ml/¹/₄ tsp salt
1 egg, beaten
200ml/7fl oz/scant 1 cup milk
15g/¹/₂oz/1 tbsp butter, melted
100ml/3¹/₂ oz/scant ¹/₂ cup strong brewed coffee
sunflower oil, for frying

For the filling

6 ripe peaches
300ml/¹/₂ pint/1¹/₄ cups double (heavy) cream
15ml/1 tbsp Amaretto liqueur
225g/8oz/1 cup mascarpone
65g/2¹/₂oz/generous ¹/₄ cup caster (superfine) sugar
30ml/2 tbsp icing (confectioners') sugar, for dusting

Sift the flours and salt into a mixing bowl. Make a well in the middle and add the egg, half the milk and the melted butter. Gradually mix in the flour, beating until smooth, then beat in the remaining milk and brewed coffee.

Heat a drizzle of oil in a 15–20cm/6–8in crêpe pan. Pour in just enough batter to thinly cover the base of the pan. Cook for about 2–3 minutes, until the underneath is golden brown, then flip over and cook the other side.

Slide the crêpe out of the pan on to a warmed plate. Continue making crêpes until all the mixture is used, stacking and interleaving with baking parchment.

To make the filling, halve the peaches and remove the stones. Cut into thick slices. Whip the cream and Amaretto liqueur until soft peaks form. Beat the mascarpone with the sugar until smooth. Beat 30ml/2 tbsp of the cream into the mascarpone, then fold in the remainder.

Spoon a little of the Amaretto cream on to one half of each pancake and top with peach slices. Gently fold the pancake over and dust with icing sugar. Serve immediately.

Energy 535kcal/2230kJ; Protein 9.6g; Carbohydrate 42.8gm, of which sugars 28.3g; Fat 37g, of which saturates 23g; Cholesterol 132.4mg; Calcium 137.3mg; Fibre 2.1g; Sodium 286mg.

TWICE-BAKED MOCHA SOUFFLÉ

The perfect way to end a meal, these mini mocha soufflés can be made up to 3 hours ahead, then reheated just before you serve them.

Serves 6

75g/3oz/6 tbsp butter, softened
90g/3½ oz plain (semisweet)
    chocolate, grated
30ml/2 tbsp ground coffee
400ml/14fl oz/1⅔ cup milk
40g/1½oz/⅓ cup plain (all-
    purpose) flour, sifted
15g/½oz/2 tbsp cocoa, sifted
3 eggs, separated
50g/2oz/¼ cup caster
    (superfine) sugar
175ml/6fl oz/¾ cup creamy
    chocolate or coffee liqueur,
    such as Crème de Caçao, or
    Sheridans

Preheat the oven to 200°C/400°F/ Gas 6. Thickly brush six 150ml/ ¼ pint/⅔ cup dariole moulds or small ovenproof bowls with 25g/1oz/ 2 tbsp of the butter. Coat with 50g/2oz of the grated chocolate.

Put the ground coffee in a small bowl. Heat the milk until almost boiling and pour over the coffee. Infuse for 4 minutes and strain, discarding the grounds.

Melt the remaining butter in a small pan. Stir in the flour and cocoa to make a roux. Cook for about 1 minute, then gradually add the coffee milk, stirring all the time to make a very thick sauce. Simmer for 2 minutes. Remove from the heat and stir in the egg yolks.

Cool for 5 minutes, then stir in the remaining chocolate. Whisk the egg whites until stiff, then gradually whisk in the sugar. Stir half into the sauce to loosen, then fold in the remainder.

Spoon the mixture into the dariole moulds and place in a roasting tin. Pour in enough hot water to come two-thirds of the way up the sides of the tins.

Bake the soufflés for 15 minutes. Turn them out on to a baking tray and leave to cool completely.

Before serving, spoon 15ml/1 tbsp chocolate or coffee liqueur over each pudding and reheat in the oven for 6–7 minutes. Serve on individual plates with the remaining liqueur poured over.

Energy 407kcal/1701kJ; Protein 8.7g; Carbohydrate 33.8gm, of which sugars 28.1g; Fat 24.3g, of which saturates 14g; Cholesterol 147.0mg; Calcium 131.5mg; Fibre 0.9g; Sodium 202mg.

VARIATION
Good quality white or milk cooking chocolate can be use instead of plain, if preferred.

RICH CHOCOLATE AND COFFEE PUDDING

A delectable blend of coffee and chocolate with a surprising layer of creamy coffee sauce underneath. Add a generous helping of whipped cream for the perfect finish.

Serves 6

75g/3oz/¾ cup plain (all-purpose) flour
10ml/2 tsp baking powder
pinch of salt
50g/2oz/¼ cup butter or margarine
25g/1oz plain (semisweet) chocolate, chopped into small pieces
115g/4oz/½ cup caster (superfine) sugar
75ml/3fl oz/5 tbsp milk
1.5ml/¼ tsp vanilla extract
whipped cream, for serving

For the topping

30ml/2 tbsp instant coffee powder
325ml/11fl oz/generous ½ pint hot water
90g/3½oz/7 tbsp soft dark brown sugar
65g/2½oz/5 tbsp caster (superfine) sugar
30ml/2 tbsp unsweetened cocoa powder, plus extra for dusting

Preheat the oven to 180°C/350°F/Gas 4. Grease a 23cm/9in square non-stick baking tin (pan).

Sift the flour, baking powder and salt into a small bowl. Set aside.

Melt the butter or margarine, chocolate and caster sugar in a heatproof bowl set over a saucepan of simmering water, or in a double boiler, stirring occasionally. Remove the bowl from the heat.

Add the flour mixture and stir well. Stir in the milk and vanilla extract. Mix with a wooden spoon, then pour the mixture into the prepared baking tin.

To make the topping, dissolve the coffee in the water in a bowl. Allow to cool. Mix the brown sugar, caster sugar and cocoa powder in a separate bowl. Sprinkle the mixture over the pudding mixture. Pour the coffee evenly over the surface.

Bake for 40 minutes or until the pudding is risen and set on top. The coffee mixture will have formed a delicious creamy sauce underneath. Serve immediately with whipped cream and dust with cocoa powder.

Energy 325kcal/1371kJ; Protein 3g; Carbohydrate 60.6g, of which sugars 50.5g; Fat 9.5g, of which saturates 5.8g; Cholesterol 19mg; Calcium 66mg; Fibre 1.1g; Sodium 107mg.

COLD COFFEE DESSERTS

WHETHER STARRING BY ITSELF OR BLENDED

WITH CHOCOLATE FOR A DARK AND LUSCIOUS

MOCHA TASTE, COFFEE IS THE PERFECT

FLAVOURING FOR THESE DELECTABLE COOLING

AFTER-DINNER TREATS

BAKED COFFEE CUSTARDS

This recipe comes from Poland, where the locals have a passion for both drinking and cooking with coffee. Here, it is used to lift a simple baked custard to new heights.

Serves 4

300ml/½ pint/1¼ cups milk
25g/1oz ground coffee (not instant)
150ml/¼ pint/⅔ cup single (light) cream
3 eggs
30ml/2 tbsp caster (superfine) sugar
whipped cream and cocoa powder, to serve

Energy 207kcal/860kJ; Protein 8.5g; Carbohydrate 12g, of which sugars 12g; Fat 14.3g, of which saturates 7.6g; Cholesterol 174mg; Calcium 147mg; Fibre 0g; Sodium 96mg.

Preheat the oven to 190°C/375°F/Gas 5. Put the milk in a heavy pan and bring to the boil. Add the coffee, remove from the heat and leave to infuse for 10 minutes. Strain the flavoured milk into a clean pan, add the cream and gently heat until just simmering.

Beat the eggs and sugar in a bowl until pale and fluffy. Pour over the hot milk mixture, whisking constantly.

Pour the custard mixture into individual heatproof bowls or coffee cups and cover tightly with foil. Place them in a roasting pan and pour in enough boiling water to come halfway up the bowls or cups.

Carefully place the roasting pan in the oven and cook for about 30 minutes, or until the custards are set. Remove from the roasting pan and leave to cool completely. Chill for at least 2 hours.

Just before serving, decorate the tops with whipped cream and dust with cocoa powder.

CLASSIC COFFEE CRÈME CARAMELS

These lightly set coffee custards are served in a pool of caramel sauce. For a richer flavour, make them with half single (light) cream, half milk.

Serves 6

600ml/1 pint/2½ cups milk
45ml/3 tbsp ground coffee
50g/2oz/¼ cup caster
  (superfine) sugar
4 eggs
4 egg yolks
spun sugar, to decorate (optional)

For the caramel sauce

150g/5oz/¾ cup caster
  (superfine) sugar
60ml/4 tbsp water

COOK'S TIP To make spun sugar, heat 75g/3oz/½ cup caster sugar, 5ml/1 tsp liquid glucose and 30ml/2 tbsp water in a pan until the sugar dissolves. Boil the syrup to 160°C/325°F, then briefly dip the base of the pan into cold water. Holding two forks together, dip them into the syrup and flick them rapidly backwards and forwards over an oiled rolling pin.

Preheat the oven to 160°C/325°F/Gas 3. To make the caramel sauce, gently heat the sugar in a small heavy-based pan with the water, until the sugar has dissolved. Bring to the boil and boil rapidly until the syrup turns a rich golden brown. Quickly and carefully, pour the hot syrup into six warmed 150ml/¼ pint/⅔ cup ramekins.

To make the coffee custard, heat the milk until almost boiling. Pour over the ground coffee and leave to infuse for about 5 minutes. Strain through a fine sieve into a jug. In a bowl, whisk the caster sugar, eggs and yolks until light and creamy. Whisk the coffee-flavoured milk into the egg mixture. Pour into the ramekins.

Put the ramekins in a roasting tin and pour in hot water to two-thirds up the sides of the dishes. Bake for 30–35 minutes or until just set. Test by gently shaking one of the custards; it should wobble like a jelly. Remove the custards from the hot water and leave to cool.

Chill the coffee custards for at least 3 hours. To turn out, carefully loosen the sides with a palette knife then invert on to serving plates. Decorate with spun sugar, if using.

Energy 284kcal/1198kJ; Protein 11.6g; Carbohydrate 39.9gm, of which sugars 39.5g; Fat 9.8g, of which saturates 3g; Cholesterol 294.3mg; Calcium 178.5mg; Fibre 0.0g; Sodium 113mg.

TIRAMISU

The name of this classic dessert translates as "pick me up", which is said to derive from the fact that it is so good that it literally makes you swoon when you eat it.

Serves 4

225g/8oz/1 cup mascarpone
25g/1oz/¼ cup icing
 (confectioners') sugar, sifted
150ml/¼ pint/⅔ cup strong
 brewed coffee, chilled
300ml/½ pint/1¼ cups
 double (heavy) cream
45ml/3 tbsp coffee liqueur such
 as Tia Maria or Kahlúa
115g/4oz Savoiardi (sponge
 finger) biscuits
50g/2oz plain (semisweet)
 chocolate, coarsely grated
cocoa powder, for dusting

> **COOK'S TIP**
> Mascarpone is a silky-textured, soft, thick cream cheese made with cow's milk.

Energy 737kcal/3055kJ; Protein 9.2g;
Carbohydrate 36.6gm, of which sugars
28.0g; Fat 60.8g, of which saturates 35g;
Cholesterol 162.8mg; Calcium 118.3mg;
Fibre 0.6g; Sodium 308mg

Lightly grease and line a 900g/2lb loaf tin (pan) with clear film. Put the mascarpone and icing sugar in a large bowl and beat for 1 minute. Stir in 30ml/2 tbsp of the chilled coffee. Mix thoroughly.

Whip the cream with 15ml/1 tbsp of the liqueur until it forms soft peaks. Stir a spoonful into the mascarpone mixture, then fold in the rest. Spoon half the mascarpone mixture into the loaf tin and smooth the top.

Put the remaining strong brewed coffee and liqueur in a shallow dish just wider than the Savoiardi biscuits. Using half the biscuits, dip one side of each biscuit into the coffee mixture, then arrange on top of the mascarpone mixture in a single layer.

Spoon the rest of the mascarpone mixture over the biscuit layer and smooth the top.

Dip the remaining biscuits in the coffee mixture, and arrange on top. Drizzle any remaining coffee mixture over the top. Cover the dish with clear film and chill for at least 4 hours.

Carefully turn the tiramisu out of the loaf tin and sprinkle with grated chocolate and cocoa powder. Serve cut into slices.

CHILLED CHOCOLATE AND ESPRESSO MOUSSE

Heady, aromatic espresso coffee adds a distinctive flavour to this smooth, rich mousse. Serve it in stylish chocolate cups for a special occasion.

Serves 4

225g/8oz plain (semisweet)
  chocolate
45ml/3 tbsp brewed espresso
25g/1oz/2 tbsp unsalted butter
4 eggs, separated
mascarpone or clotted cream,
  to serve (optional)
sprigs of fresh mint, to
  decorate (optional)

For the chocolate cups

225g/8oz plain (semisweet)
  chocolate

Energy 721kcal/3012kJ; Protein 13.2g;
Carbohydrate 71.5gm, of which sugars
70.4g; Fat 44.4g, of which saturates 25g;
Cholesterol 255.3mg; Calcium 72.8mg;
Fibre 2.8g; Sodium 92mg.

For each chocolate cup, cut a double thickness 15cm/6in square of foil. Mould it around a small orange, leaving the edges and corners loose to make a cup shape. Remove the orange and press the bottom of the foil case gently on a surface to make a flat base. Repeat to make four individual foil cups.

Break the plain chocolate into small pieces and place in a bowl set over a pan of very hot water. Stir occasionally until the chocolate has melted.

Spoon the chocolate into the foil cups, spreading it up the sides with the back of a spoon to give a ragged edge. Refrigerate for 30 minutes or until set hard. Gently peel away the foil, starting at the top edge.

To make the chocolate mousse, put the plain chocolate and brewed espresso into a bowl set over a pan of hot water and melt as before. When it is smooth and liquid, add the unsalted butter, a little at a time. Remove the pan from the heat then stir in the egg yolks.

Whisk the egg whites in a bowl until stiff, but not dry, then fold them into the chocolate mixture. Pour into a bowl and refrigerate for at least 3 hours.

To serve, scoop the chilled mousse into the chocolate cups. Add a scoop of mascarpone or clotted cream and decorate with a sprig of fresh mint, if you wish.

MOCHA, PRUNE AND ARMAGNAC TERRINES

A really simple iced dessert that is perfect for entertaining. Just remember to allow time for the prunes to soak in the Armagnac.

Serves 6

*115g/4oz/½ cup ready-to-eat
  pitted prunes, chopped
90ml/6 tbsp Armagnac
90g/3½oz/½ cup caster
  (superfine) sugar
150ml/¼ pint/⅔ cup water
45ml/3 tbsp coffee beans
150g/5oz plain (semisweet)
  chocolate, broken into pieces
300ml/½ pint/1¼ cups
  double (heavy) cream
cocoa powder, for dusting*

Put the prunes in a small bowl. Pour over 75ml/5 tbsp of the Armagnac and leave to soak for at least 3 hours at room temperature, or overnight in the refrigerator. Line the bases of six 100ml/3½fl oz/scant ½ cup ramekins with circles cut from baking parchment.

Put the sugar and the measured water in a heavy-based pan and heat gently until the sugar dissolves, stirring occasionally. Add the soaked prunes and any of the Armagnac that remains in the bowl; simmer the prunes gently in the syrup for 5 minutes.

Using a slotted spoon, lift the prunes out of the pan and set them aside. Add the coffee beans to the syrup and simmer gently for 5 minutes.

Lift out the coffee beans and put about a third of them in a bowl. Spoon over 120ml/4fl oz/½ cup of the syrup and stir in the remaining Armagnac.

Add the chocolate to the pan containing the remaining syrup and leave until melted. Whip the cream until it just holds its shape. Using a large metal spoon, fold the chocolate mixture and prunes into the cream until just combined. Spoon the mixture into the lined ramekins, cover and freeze for at least 3 hours.

To serve, loosen the edges of the ramekins with a knife then dip in very hot water for 2 seconds and invert on to serving plates. Decorate the plates with coffee bean syrup and cocoa powder.

Energy 100kcal/419kJ; Protein 0.9g; Carbohydrate 10.1g, of which sugars 9.9g; Fat 6.3g, of which saturates 3.8g; Cholesterol 8mg; Calcium 10mg; Fibre 0.8g; Sodium 7mg.

COOK'S TIP
Both the individual terrines and the coffee bean syrup can be made several days in advance if you want to save last-minute cooking. Cover the syrup and store it in the refrigerator.

GINGERED COFFEE MERINGUES

What could be more enticing than to break through the coating of crisp meringue to reveal just-melting coffee ice cream on a moist ginger sponge?

Serves 6

275g/10oz bought ginger cake
600ml/1 pint/2½ cups coffee
*   ice cream*
4 egg whites
1.5ml/¼ tsp cream of tartar
150g/5oz/¾ cup caster
*   (superfine) sugar*
25g/1oz/2 tbsp preserved stem
*   ginger, finely chopped*

> **COOK'S TIP**
> The ice cream is insulated in the oven by the tiny bubbles of air in the meringue, so ensure it is completely covered. Once coated, the ice cream cakes could be frozen until ready to cook.

Energy 460kcal/1939kJ; Protein 8.1g; Carbohydrate 78.0gm, of which sugars 66.7g; Fat 15.0g, of which saturates 9g; Cholesterol 26.0mg; Calcium 138.3mg; Fibre 0.4g; Sodium 277mg.

Preheat the oven to 230°C/450°F/Gas 8. Cut the ginger cake lengthways into three slices. Stamp out two rounds from each slice, using a 5cm/2in cutter, and put on a baking tray.

Top each cake round with a large scoop of coffee ice cream, then place the baking tray in the freezer for at least 30 minutes.

Whisk the egg whites and cream of tartar until soft peaks form. Gradually add the sugar and continue whisking until the mixture forms stiff peaks. Fold in the preserved ginger.

Carefully spoon the meringue and ginger mixture into a piping bag fitted with a large plain nozzle.

Quickly pipe the meringue over the ice cream, starting from the base and working up to the top.

Bake in the oven for 3–4 minutes, until the outside of the meringue is crisp and lightly tinged with brown. Serve immediately.

COFFEE GRANITA

The most famous of all granitas, this originated in Mexico. It consists of full-bodied coffee frozen into tiny ice flakes. It tastes sensational on its own or served with cream.

Serves 6

75ml/5 tbsp good quality ground filter coffee
1 litre/1¾ pints/4 cups boiling water
150g/5oz/¾ cup caster (superfine) sugar
150ml/¼ pint/⅔ cup double (heavy) cream (optional)

COOK'S TIP

If you taste the coffee before freezing, don't be alarmed by its strength; the change from liquid to ice mysteriously dulls the flavour, so the finished taste is just right.

Spoon the coffee into a cafetière (press pot) or jug (pitcher), pour on the boiling water and leave to stand for 5 minutes. Plunge the cafetière or strain from the jug. Pour the coffee into a large plastic container, to a maximum depth of 2.5cm/1in.

Add the sugar and stir until it has dissolved completely. Leave the mixture to cool.

Cover and freeze for 2 hours or until the coffee mixture around the sides of the container is starting to become mushy.

Using a fork, break up the ice crystals and mash the mixture finely. Return the granita to the freezer for 2 hours more, beating every 30 minutes until the ice becomes fine, even crystals.

After the final beating return the now slushy granita to the freezer. When ready to serve, spoon the granita into glass dishes. Whip the cream and offer it separately, if you like.

Energy 102kcal/434kJ; Protein 0.5g; Carbohydrate 26.6gm, of which sugars 26.1g; Fat 0.0g, of which saturates 0g; Cholesterol 0.0mg; Calcium 12.3mg; Fibre 0.0g; Sodium 3mg.

COFFEE CREAM PROFITEROLES

Crisp-textured coffee choux pastry puffs are filled with cream and drizzled with a white chocolate sauce. For those with a sweet tooth, there is plenty of extra sauce.

Serves 6

65g/2½oz/9 tbsp plain (all-purpose) white flour
pinch of salt
50g/2oz/4 tbsp butter
150ml/¼ pint/⅔ cup brewed coffee
2 eggs, lightly beaten

For the white chocolate sauce

50g/2oz/¼ cup sugar
100ml/3½fl oz/scant ½ cup water
150g/5oz good quality white chocolate, broken into pieces
25g/1oz/2 tbsp butter
45ml/3 tbsp double (heavy) cream
30ml/2 tbsp coffee liqueur, such as Tia Maria, Kahlúa or Toussaint

For the filling

250ml/8fl oz/1 cup double (heavy) cream

Preheat the oven to 220°C/425°F/Gas 7. Sift the flour and salt on to a piece of baking parchment. Cut the butter into pieces and put in a pan with the coffee.

Bring to a rolling boil, then remove from the heat and tip in all the flour. Beat until the mixture leaves the sides of the pan. Leave to cool for 2 minutes.

Gradually add the eggs, beating well between each addition. Spoon the mixture into a piping bag fitted with a 1cm/½in plain nozzle.

Pipe about 24 small buns on to a dampened baking sheet. Bake for 20 minutes, until well risen and crisp.

Remove the buns from the oven and pierce the side of each with a sharp knife to let out the steam.

To make the sauce, put the sugar and water in a heavy-based pan and heat gently until dissolved. Bring to the boil and simmer for 3 minutes. Remove from the heat. Add the chocolate and butter, stirring until smooth. Stir in the cream and liqueur.

To assemble, whip the cream until soft peaks form. Using a piping bag, fill the choux buns through the slits in the sides. Arrange on plates and pour a little of the sauce over, either warm or at room temperature. Serve the remaining sauce separately.

Energy 592kcal/2455kJ; Protein 6.5g; Carbohydrate 33.9gm, of which sugars 25.6g; Fat 47.5g, of which saturates 29g; Cholesterol 173.8mg; Calcium 123.5mg; Fibre 0.3g; Sodium 119mg.

FROSTED RASPBERRY AND COFFEE TERRINE

A white chocolate and fresh raspberry layer and a contrasting smooth coffee layer make this attractive looking dessert doubly delicious.

Serves 6–8

30ml/2 tbsp ground coffee,
250ml/8fl oz/1 cup milk
4 eggs, separated
50g/2oz/¼ cup caster
   (superfine) sugar
30ml/2 tbsp cornflour
   (cornstarch)
150ml/¼ pint/⅔ cup double
   (heavy) cream
150g/5oz white chocolate,
   roughly chopped
115g/4oz/⅔ cup raspberries
shavings of white chocolate and
   cocoa powder, to decorate

COOK'S TIP

After decorating, allow the terrine to soften in the refrigerator for 20 minutes before slicing and serving.

Energy 285kcal/1189kJ; Protein 6.2g;
Carbohydrate 23.4g, of which sugars
19.9g; Fat 19.2g, of which saturates
10.8g; Cholesterol 123mg; Calcium
119mg; Fibre 0.4g; Sodium 76mg.

Line a 1.5 litre/2½ pint/6¼ cup loaf tin with clear film and put in the freezer to chill. Put the ground coffee in a jug (pitcher). Heat 100ml/3½fl oz/scant ½ cup of the milk to near-boiling point and pour over the coffee. Leave to infuse.

Blend the egg yolks, sugar and cornflour together in a pan and whisk in the remaining milk and the cream. Bring to the boil, stirring all the time, until thickened.

Divide the hot mixture between two bowls and add the white chocolate to one, stirring until melted. Strain the coffee through a fine sieve (strainer) into the other bowl and mix well. Leave until cool, stirring occasionally.

Whisk two of the egg whites until stiff. Fold into the coffee custard. Spoon into the tin and freeze for 30 minutes.

Whisk remaining whites and fold into the chocolate mixture with the raspberries. Spoon into the tin and level before freezing for 4 hours.

Turn the terrine out on to a flat serving plate and peel off the clear film. Cover with chocolate shavings and dust with cocoa powder.

ESPRESSO-HAZELNUT BALLS

Marzipan is a wonderful vehicle for other flavours. The bitterness of good fresh coffee or espresso ground together with the warmth of toasted hazelnuts is always a good combination.

Makes 24 balls

200g/7oz good store-bought marzipan
50g/2oz hazelnuts, toasted and chopped
25ml/1½ tbsp cold espresso or strong coffee
5ml/1 tsp fresh espresso grounds
2.5ml/½ tsp cognac or Grand Marnier
caster (superfine) sugar, for rolling

Energy 45kcal/ 186kJ; Protein 0.8g; Carbohydrate 3.6g, of which sugars 3.5g; Fat 3g, of which saturates 0.2g; Cholesterol 0mg; Calcium 9mg; Fibre 0.3g; Sodium 1mg.

Put all of the ingredients except the caster sugar into a large bowl and mix together with clean hands.

Divide the mixture into 24 pieces and roll into balls.

Pour some sugar on to a plate and roll the balls around in it – you will need to do this in a couple of batches.

Serve immediately, or store, covered, for up to 2 weeks in the refrigerator.

COFFEE STUFFED PRUNES

Chocolate-covered prunes, soaked in liqueur, hide a melt-in-the-mouth coffee filling.
Fresh dates can be used instead of prunes, if preferred.

Makes 30

*225g/8oz/1 cup unpitted
prunes
50ml/2fl oz/¼ cup Armagnac
30ml/2 tbsp ground coffee
150ml/¼ pint/⅔ cup double
(heavy) cream
350g/12oz bittersweet or plain
chocolate, broken into
squares
30ml/2 tbsp cocoa powder,
for dusting*

Put the prunes in a bowl and pour over the Armagnac. Stir, cover with clear film (plastic wrap) and set aside for 2 hours so the liquid is absorbed. Make a slit along each prune to remove the stone, making a hollow for the filling, but leaving the fruit intact.

Put the coffee and cream in a pan and heat almost to boiling point. Cover, infuse for 4 minutes, then heat again until almost boiling. Put 115g/4oz of the chocolate into a bowl and pour over the coffee cream.

Stir until the chocolate has melted and the mixture is smooth. Leave to cool, until it has the consistency of softened butter.

Fill a piping bag with a small nozzle with the chocolate mixture. Pipe into the cavities of the prunes. Chill in the refrigerator for 20 minutes.

Melt the remaining chocolate in a bowl over a pan of hot water. Using a fork, dip the prunes into the chocolate to coat. Place on non-stick baking parchment to harden. Dust each with a little cocoa powder.

Energy 100kcal/419kJ; Protein 0.9g;
Carbohydrate 10.1g, of which sugars
9.9g; Fat 6.3g, of which saturates 3.8g;
Cholesterol 8mg; Calcium 10mg; Fibre
0.8g; Sodium 7mg.

INDEX